Cultural Issues
in
Business Communication

Second Edition

Robert G. Sellin
Elaine Winters

For additional copies or reproduction information, contact:

Elaine Winters, ewinters@ewinters.com
Robert G. Sellin, rsellin@ostrans.com

Printed by BOOKSURGE Publishing

Book design by Elaine Winters and
Marla Wilson, Printed Page Productions
Berkeley, California.

CONTENTS

Preface

Our world changes quickly.

Communicators have the responsibility to be pace setters in sharing information and articulating ideas with as few misunderstandings as possible.

This Guide offers insights and techniques to help in the fulfillment of that responsibility. This guide does not (and should not) attempt to prescribe specific communication strategies for each "culture."

Our goal is to help you ask the right questions and develop sensitivities to cultural requirements that arise as you participate in moving information around the world.

Increasingly, businesses communicate in different languages and via several media. The opportunity to communicate information across cultures is facilitated by knowing and respecting the needs of your translator and your customer/end user.

As an informed and aware communicator you will make allowances for cultural accommodation. You will save time, effort, and contribute to your company's success and profitability, as well as add to your own enjoyment as you travel the world.

We write this Guide in the interest of improved communication and with the sincere hope that better communication will lead to enhanced understanding in our changing world.

©1996–2005 Robert G. Sellin and Elaine Winters
Berkeley, California, U.S.A.

This English preface is translated into three languages: French, Japanese, and Spanish. Translator's comments follow each translation.

Avant-propos

Dans ce monde en évolution rapide, il incombe aux communicateurs de donner le ton en transmettant l'information et en articulant les idées avec le moins d'équivoque possible.

Ce guide offre des points de repère et des techniques destinées à faciliter cette tâche. Cependant, il ne saurait essayer de prescrire des stratégies de communication particulières pour chaque culture.

Notre objectif est simplement de vous aider à vous poser les bonnes questions et de vous sensibiliser aux impératifs culturels des échanges d'information internationaux.

On assiste actuellement à une multiplication des langues et des moyens de communication utilisés par les entreprises. La bonne communication entre les cultures est facilitée par la compréhension et le respect des besoins de vos traducteurs, de vos clients et des utilisateurs de vos produits ou services.

En communicateur averti, vous tiendrez compte de ces adaptations culturelles. Cela vous procurera un gain de temps et d'efforts qui favorisera le succès et le rendement de votre entreprise, ainsi que votre épanouissement personnel tandis que vous parcourez le monde.

Nous avons conçu ce guide pour promouvoir une meilleure communication qui, nous l'espérons du fond du cœur, conduira à l'entente mutuelle dans ce monde en mutation.

© Robert G. Sellin et Elaine Winters, 1996, 2005
Berkeley (Californie)

French Translator Comments

Readers who can read French will notice that the translation often strives for conciseness, using formulations that differ significantly from the English text. Trying to preserve the literal content and structure of English sentences in a French translation generally results in an unbearably bloated style. Attempting to point out and describe each and every difference in formulation would result in a fairly long essay in comparative semantics and stylistics, and the use of advanced specialized terminology. The comments below point out only a few examples of these differences without resorting to a complex linguistic analysis.

1. "Preface" was replaced with "Foreword" *(Avant-propos)*. French readers would expect a preface to be a longer, more developed analysis.

2. The two first sentences were merged into one. A French reader would consider the first statement as fairly trivial and would prefer to see the connection between the two juxtaposed statements made explicit.

3. The translation of "communicators have the responsibility to..." *(il incombe aux communicateurs de...)* can be read as "it rests on communicators to" or "it is incumbent upon communicators to". This formulation will sound more idiomatic in French and not as "formal" as in English.

4. "To be pace setters" is translated by "to set the tone" *(Donner le ton)*. The figurative sense of "pace setting" needs to be made explicit in the French text. A direct translation of "to set the pace" could convey the idea

that "communicators should hurry to share information".

5. There is no direct translation of "insight" in French, but rather a choice of possible translations requiring a careful selection based on context and intent. Here we chose to go with a translation equivalent to "reference point".

6. "Does not (and should not) attempt to". French offers a more synthetic form to mean all that: *ne saurait essayer de*. Based on the negative conditional form of a verb meaning "to know" ("would not know how to…"), this expression really means something like "could not and/or wouldn't dare to".

7. "Develop sensitivities" is translated by the verb *sensibiliser* ("to increase awareness").

8. "Requirements that arise as you participate in moving information" is translated as *impératifs des échanges d'information* ("requirements of information exchanges"), for the sake of conciseness. Does this result in any significant information loss?

9. "Increasingly…" For French readers, the fact that companies may have to work in different languages and through several media is already a given. For that reason, the translation needs to emphasize the multiplication of the languages and media being used.

10. "Informed and aware". In French, one word is enough: *averti*.

11. "Enjoyment" is rendered by *épanouissement,* which adds the idea of "personal development" (literally "blossoming") over mere "pleasure".

12. Note that the copyright reference is ordered differently in French.

13. The vast majority of French-speaking people do not need to be reminded that California is part of the United States. In general, French readers do not like to be told things that they consider obvious. Redundancies and repetitions usually make them cringe.

Thierry Chambon
Sarasota, Florida

序文

世界は急速に変化しています。

コミュニケーション産業に携わる皆様は、情報を交換しアイディアを表現する際、できる限り誤解をなくすためのペースセッターとなる使命がおありになることと存じます。

本ガイド書はそのような使命を全うする皆様のお役に立つことを願い、見識、テクニックを記載致しております。本書はそれぞれの「文化」におけるある特定のコミュニケーション手段を提供するものではありませんし、そのような意図もありません。

世界の情報交換に参加する際、相応の質問をし、持ち上がってくる文化的必要事項を十分に考慮できる手助けができればと考えております。

ビジネス界において、異なる言語でのさまざまなメディアによるコミュニケーションは増えております。異文化間における情報交換の機会は翻訳者やお客様・エンドユーザーの方々のニーズを知り、貢献することで促進できます。

異なる文化の知識を持ち、関心を抱くことでそれらの文化への順応が容易になります。それにより皆様の時間、努力を削減でき、また、貴社の業績、プロフィットにも貢献することになります。また、世界を旅したときの個人の楽しみも増すことでしょう。

コミュニケーション促進に貢献したく、また、より効果的なコミュニケーションにより、この変化する世界を理解するお役に立ちたいとの願いがこの本書となりました。

1996－2005 ロブ セリンとイレーヌ ウィンターズ
合衆国カリフォルニア州、バークレー

本書はフランス語、日本、スペイン語に訳されております。翻訳の後に翻訳者のコメントが付いております。

Japanese Translator Comments

The word 'help' in the second paragraph was translated as support because it better communicated the notion of the sentence. Phonetically in Japanese: supporto.

The phrase 'saving effort' was questioned by the translator. Effort in the Japanese culture is a main virtue (the three main virtues being: patience, effort, and perseverance). Therefore 'saving effort' might sound lazy to a Japanese person. So, the word effort was changed to energy in order to preserve the original meaning.

Sensitive was actually explained, using several characters, and spelled phonetically.

Words were added to communicate a higher level of politeness.

Kikuyo Matsumoto Power
Mercer Island, Washington

Prefacio

Nuestro mundo evoluciona con rapidez.

Recae sobre los profesionales de la comunicación la responsabilidad de ser quienes marcan el ritmo del intercambio de información, y de articular las ideas con tan pocos malentendidos como sea posible.

Esta guía ofrece al lector percepciones y técnicas para ayudarle en el descargo de esta responsabilidad. No intenta – y no sería apropiado que intentara – ser prescriptiva en cuanto a estrategias específicas para comunicarse con cada "cultura".

Nuestro objetivo es ayudarle a hacer las preguntas acertadas y a desarrollar sensibilidad por los requisitos culturales que vayan surgiendo a medida que participa en el movimiento de información alrededor del mundo.

Más y más, las empresas se comunican en distintos idiomas valiéndose de varios medios. Esa oportunidad de transmitir información a través de diversas culturas será tanto más fácil de aprovechar si conoce y respeta las necesidades de su traductor y las de su cliente o usuario final.

Como profesional de la comunicación informado y consciente, tendrá en cuenta que – de antemano – hay que proveer cierto margen para que una cultura no desencaje con otra. Economizará tiempo y esfuerzo, contribuirá al éxito y rentabilidad de su empresa y, además, a medida que viaja por el mundo, podrá disfrutar de la experiencia cada vez más.

Escribimos esta Guía con el ánimo de mejorar las comunicaciones y la esperanza de que una mejor comunicación conducirá hacia una mayor comprensión en el cambiante mundo que compartimos.

Nota de la traductora

Texts of a literary nature lends themselves to countless nuances of interpretation, which you resolve when you edit the final draft and often under pressure, as the looming deadline forces us to settle on this or that version of an utterance that we would rather keep analyzing and perfecting.

The Spanish language characteristically employs a higher register than English in texts of this nature, a source of constant tension for the translator caught between the poles of fidelity to the source and fidelity to the natural tendencies of the target language.

Spanish is very sparing in the use of personal pronouns, possessives, and passive sentence constructions. The translator has to decide when to use the pronouns "you" and "your" purely for emphasis, and that's to make the reader feel personally appealed to, involved, or responsible for something, as the writer may have intended. If you look at the 3rd paragraph, there are two "yous", but their function is not emphasis, they are just necessary in English. The first one is reflected obliquely in Spanish in the proclictic pronoun "le" in "ayudarle" and the second elided, as is usual. In "your translator and your customer" where the authors have addressed the reader as an individual, the use of the possessive in Spanish, rather than the article (el traductor y el cliente) is deliberate, and justified by the authors' switch from the general to the particular.

In the case of passive sentence constructions, of "the tail was wagged by the dog" kind, while our training reminds us to revert to the active construction, you have to ask yourself if the writer, consciously or not, put the object before the subject to underline its importance, since studies have shown that the first clause has more impact than the last.

The second sentence of Paragraph 4 presents two dilemmas in one: "The opportunity to communicate information across cultures is facilitated by knowing and respecting the needs of your translator and your customer/end user." Despite the verb form, it's not really a passive construction, is it? After playing with the inverse order of the clauses, many formulas were tried to leave the key words in place in more or less the same order of appearance, for the sake of fidelity of emphasis, and my solution entailed using a "you" that was not there in English: Esa oportunidad que usted tiene de transmitir información a través de diversas culturas será tanto más fácil de aprovechar si conoce y respeta las necesidades de su traductor y las de su cliente o usuario final. Now, having met my goal of fidelity by personalizing the clause, I could and did go back and elide the pronoun and verb: "Esa oportunidad de transmitir información a través de diversas culturas será tanto más fácil..." The second problem is still the subject, opportunity. In Spanish you could not say "The opportunity... is facilitated by" even though the verb facilitar exists, so the cognate fácil was woven into a phrase, fácil de aprovechar, which completed the internal logic for the Spanish reader.

To mention one final example of cultural or idiomatic adaptation, the word sincere was dropped from the 6th paragraph, because esperanza, by itself, has more impact –and says it all—whereas sincera esperanza is not natural: conversely, are there insincere hopes in Spanish? There are false hopes, naive hopes, humble ones and desperate hopes, yes, but they are all sincere by definition, which in Spanish makes the use of the adjective redundant, so it was eliminated to allow the noun its true value. Strangely, the result reflects the humility with which the hope was offered!

Sylvia Korwek
Walnut Creek, California

Summary

These three seemingly simple and brief translation examples and associated translator comments illuminate the translation process. They demonstrate how easily misunderstandings might arise. Clearly your translator and instructional designer must be chosen with great care. Note, too, the physical space required by each language to communicate the same content.

Linguistic and cultural audits should be integral to language translation.

INTRODUCTION

Our study of, and experience in, cross-cultural communication remains a life-long pursuit. In this spirit we add, in this second edition, our insights and suggestions based on our varied experience and study over the five years since the publication of the first edition.

The compilation of this information began as a series of conference presentations, then migrated to the Internet, and then became the first edition of this book. Since then, Robert has returned from sailing across the Pacific to Australia, and Elaine has lived and worked in Europe.

The first sections of this book discuss numerous issues that arise as we attempt to make thoughts, needs, and information known across cultures, such as:

- building relationships
- formality/informality
- decision making

Later, we consider more practical matters:

- document design
- writing for translation
- managing translation (process and resources)
- the internet and how it influences the translation process and communication, generally

We also provide some specific instructions for getting through mechanical tasks that require judgement calls.

Finally, we offer a few published articles, written by Elaine, that speak to many of these issues as well as some observations about global roaming.

We are fully aware that this is not a complete treatment of the complex subject of cross-cultural communication. This is our attempt to raise issues, provide some practical instruction, and share a few checklists for helping solve some of the many challenges that people typically encounter as cultures cross.

We are always learning and interested in feedback. Please share your comments and suggestions with us.

Thank you.

Robert G. Sellin: rsellin@ostrans.com
Elaine Winters: ewinters@ewinters.com

Berkeley, California
U.S.A.

1 CULTURE AND INFORMATION PRESENTATION

Developing communications in today's international business environment generally involves a team or group process. The best way to "take care of business" is when a few people meet and work together in person.

Increasingly however, business decisions are made and information is created and processed by the efforts of members of a virtual team—that is a work group whose members are often in different geographical locations and from different cultures.

With the proliferation of email, instant messaging, secure intranets, video conferencing, the ubiquitous fax machine, and the telephone, virtual teaming is on the increase. Using these communication tools increases the potential for misunderstanding between team members, as compared with working together in person. In person you can observe body language, evaluate pauses, note inflections, and share other important information. Learning how to work as the member of a cross cultural virtual team has become an important skill.

How efficiently and effectively people get along with one another, respect each others ideas, and resolve their inevitable professional and personal differences can determine the difference between success and failure.

How can we learn about one another, begin to ask questions, and make the kind of observations that will make understanding each other easier and more successful? How can we learn to better appreciate the "culture" of a co-worker, a working group, or a company?

Anthropologists have developed some definitions and ways of observing cultures that can prove useful when working in a team comprised of people from different countries, ethnic groups, and linguistic biases. Let's look at two of these: low and high context.[1]

Low- and High- context Cultures

Low-context cultures—roughly, the native English speakers, Scandinavians, and those speaking German, and linguistically similar dialects—expect a high level of detail in their visual, verbal, and written communication. All the information is expected to be in what is directly and immediately communicated. The communication is contained, mainly, in the words and images themselves.

High-context cultures—roughly, everyone else—pay a lot of attention to surrounding details and the totality of the content and context, for example:

- physical location
- ambiance
- verbal tone
- clothing or attire
- the individual
- the institution

This attention to content can enhance or detract from information not obtained during in-person, print,

---

1. These terms and concepts are fully explained in the writings of Dr. Edward T. Hall, specifically, in *Beyond Culture*.

multimedia, or other forms of information acquisition. At the very least, these factors can add to the information in unintentional ways and increase the possibility of misunderstanding.

Concepts of time and its importance vary from culture to culture, as do relationships and their place in the culture of a business environment. These concepts and relationships must be ascertained in and for each situation. Each cultural setting has a 'signature'—a specific ambiance, *requiring* definition, respect, and attention. If it is something you need assistance with, ask colleagues when necessary.

Examples:

> North Americans have their unique way of defining a business relationship, such as "Let's do lunch". Find out what it is for the particular cultural situation in which you find yourself, and try not to violate the formality, or lack thereof. Ask about what you don't understand or when you are confused by what you're experiencing.

> The Japanese, among others, tend to want to build relationships before getting down to business. This can take two hours, when you are a known quantity. It can take years if no one has ever heard of you, particularly if 'no one' anybody knows or trusts has sent a letter or telephoned with information about you. In other words: 'who sent you' is a serious factor.

> North Americans like to get things done quickly with a memo, fax, or an email (cut to the chase). That may not be acceptable everywhere.

> Can you answer this question: What is the
> accepted form for written communication for
> your colleagues?

Similarly, what is the correct form and time for telephone
conversations? Some countries take *siesta*; it would be
considered rude to telephone just as people are leaving
the office for a long leisurely lunch and an afternoon
nap. Insisting on meeting at one thirty in the afternoon in
these countries is similarly considered rude and
insensitive.

For meetings with colleagues and/or customers,
answering the following series of questions might be
valuable and instructive:

- Who makes the decision about where and when a
  meeting will be held?
- Who chairs the meeting?
- Who sets the agenda?
- How can you best ascertain if there is a hidden
  agenda and what it is?
- What are the expectations for seating
  arrangements? Will everyone face each other or sit
  in a row with a leader in front of the room?
- Are gifts expected? By whom? What is
  appropriate?
- What company policy must you be aware of?
- Are all members of the team similarly advised?
- Which names are appropriate?
- How do people wish to be addressed? Formally?
  Informally? First names?

- Are name tags appropriate? If so, which colors are appropriate? More importantly, which colors are inappropriate?

Add your unique considerations to this list. Take into account what you already know about the target culture.

2   SIMILARITIES AND DIFFERENCES

L'ESCANT[2] is the acronym David Victor developed as the mnemonic for the similarities and differences in cultures. We use it here as a tool for thinking about cross-cultural communication issues.

As you gain experience, you may want to develop your own tools to perform better audience identification markers. (Call it an international audit device, an inventory, or whatever you feel comfortable with.)

It may be useful to think of the similarities and differences in terms of the following:

- individual
- organization
- nation-state

Each of the following categories is a starting place. For each environment you will find additions.

L'ESCANT Described

L/anguage

Official languages and dialects. For example, Singapore has four official languages: English, Mandarin, Malay, and Tamil, and dialects of each.

---

2. LESCANT= Language, Environment, Social Organization, Context, Authority Conception, Non-verbal behavior, Time

Is the population bi- or multi-lingual? How is the style of writing usually characterized in a defined situation? When is formality expected?

When is it appropriate to use an informal mode? When and what kind of humor is appropriate?

E/nvironment and Technology

As time goes on these are increasingly important and some aspects of your communication that did not take these issues into consideration a few year ago, may need to be revisited and reevaluated.

- What are the educational /environmental factors, such as the generally accepted body of knowledge, teaching style (traditional or modern)?
- What is the literacy rate in the environment in which you'll be working, and in the country generally?
- What are the technological variables?
- What is the availability or capabilities of the telephone system?
- Do many people have access to computers? Are computers generally available to the public—in libraries, for example?
- What is the level of computer literacy? (Try rating the sophistication of your population on a scale of one to ten with one representing one telephone for 500,000 people and proportionately few computers.)

Other technologies that may differ include electrical outlet configuration and AC voltage/cycles.

Computer keyboards and operating systems differ to accommodate character sets, punctuation, and symbols.

S/ocial Organization

Each society arranges itself differently. Answering the following list of questions may provide some insight into the community you find youself involved with.

- What is the accepted social etiquette of business in less formal and on non-formal occasions?
- What are the family values in these societies?
- Can you identify prejudices, such as attitudes toward aging, leisure time, and outsiders?
- Is the society structured with large extended families that tend to live near each other and work together for common goals?
- Is it composed of relatively small nuclear families that tend to not band together?

C/ontext

- What is the context of your interaction?
- Is it partly business, partly social, all business, or only social?
- What are the rules for each? Both?
- When are they mixed?
- What are the rules for gender interaction?
- What is the prevailing management style?
- Which management styles do your colleagues or customers prefer?

A/uthority Conception

- Who is in charge, and why?
- What economic factors influence authority?
- How is age a factor in determining authority?
- What are the varieties of currency?
- Do favors count as a clearly defined substitute for money?
- What is the definition of wealth?
- How is status determined?

N/onverbal Behavior

- How do people stand when they talk to one another?
- What are the accepted seating arrangements—business and social?
- Are there generally accepted religious principles that cannot be violated, such as certain foods (accepted or taboo), colors, icons, and particular forbidden behaviors?
- What are the political traditions concerning:
  - trade (for example, is barter part of the shared history?)
  - legal (what is justice, how is it carried out, and who decides?)
  - symbols (are there ones that must be respected and acknowledged?)
- Which hand gestures are acceptable?
- What do various items of apparel communicate?

T/ime

- Is time analogous with money or is it relative and non-ending?
- Is it used differently for relationship building within the context of business?
- Is time treated the same in all contexts, both business and personal, with adults and children?
- Do people arrive for appointments at the designated time or is there a different standard?
- Do buses and trains follow a strict schedule that can be depended on?
- What time conventions are in effect during holidays?

Source:
Victor, Dav.d: *International Business Communication*, AddisonWesley, 1992.

3   Document Design

When planning document design, consider the variety of culturally sensitive issues we mention in this section. Our goal is to help you create and select designs appropriate to the target cultures. We list a few issues for you to consider including page layout, alphabet fonts, character sets, and publishing requirements. Make your own checklist to fit your situation and documents.

Page Layout, Fonts and Character Sets

Page Design: Whether or not a document has an esthetically pleasing design is culturally linked. Find out the expectations of your audience.

In the target culture, what are the design characteristics of:

- books
- magazines
- newspapers
- brochures

How are cartoons and graphics drawn and used?

Alphabet sizes: Different alphabets and character sets take up different physical space.

One accommodating method is to use a larger font in the original (or source language), which provides a bit of flexibility when translating into a language that uses more physical space (up to 25% more space, in some cases) in a given text, graphic, or numeric field. Also, leave white space on the page for this text expansion. Graphics should contain numbered call-outs, instead of text, with an easily modified legend outside the graphic.

Fonts or Character sets: Get samples of fonts, as well as bullets and dingbats from your translator before work begins. Make sure they are what you want.

Sync: Graphics and text can be uncoordinated (out of sync) on the page.

Solve this by dividing pages into columns and having one column for graphics and another for text. The positions of both can then be adjusted to the various alphabets and different writing systems. This can be automated on some word processors. Too narrow a column can be a problem for documents translated into German, the Scandinavian, and the Pacific island languages.

Provide metric equivalents for all measurements.

Orientation: Which way is the text going to be read: left to right, right to left, or vertically? Some languages (Japanese) can be read R-L, L-R, and vertically. Classic examples of R-L are Arabic and Hebrew.

Paper Size: Which size to use? The U.S. typically uses 8.5 x 11 inch paper. Most countries use A4 paper (210 x 297 mm). When setting up word processing, or instructing translators and print vendors, design your project to accommodate this requirement. One American company printed brochures on 8.5 x 11 inch stock for an international trade show, only to find out that they would not fit into the on-site brochure holders.

Color: Color considerations are many and sometimes complex. Here are a few examples of color associations within different cultures:

Red   *China*: prosperity/good fortune
         Ivory Coast: mourning
         Malaysia: strength
         North American: stop

Green   *many countries*: environmental awareness
         Muslims: associated with Mohammed
         North American: go/start

Blue   *Ghana*: joy/happiness
         Native American: hope/religious significance

Yellow   *Malaysia*: royalty
         North America: caution
         China: wealth

When using color in a graphic presentation, a title or headline can be in black for easy and less expensive modification.

Publishing Requirements

When you are designing your documents, take into account the publishing process and requirements of the document and of the publisher or print vendor. Some of the issues to consider are as follows:

- page specifications
- treatment of text expansion
- platform compatibility
- publication medium and device

- treatment of graphics, supplying artwork
- screen shots, when applicable

Corporate guidelines also must be communicated.

When working with European languages, it is tempting to replace the source text in a Pagemaker, Quark, or FrameMaker file, with the translated text to retain the document layout. Be certain that the punctuation conventions are *not* retained as well

Chinese and Japanese are the primary Asian languages using character sets rather than alphabets. Character sets come in many styles. So deciding on the style is important. You can best view the translation and page formatting as a PDF. Once the PDF draft is approved it should be saved as an EPS. The outlined characters are thus saved as a graphic (which can be scaled) by an application such as Adobe Illustrator®. These EPS files can then be imported into your print vendor's publishing/printing application.

Be certain of what is required and communicate this to your translator. Any incompatibilities must be resolved at the outset.

4   INFORMATION ORGANIZATION

How we view information is directly linked to considerations about what is important and in what context it is important. Those are all cultural considerations.

One approach is to organize material alphabetically. Another is to organize by discreet modules—small booklets, job aids, or manuals that each address only one need. Examples are:

- programmer guides
- user guides
- reference booklets

Most material designed and written in North America is targeted at the 'do it now!' American/Western (mainly), white male audience. Yes, that's changing.

Understanding your audience requirements *before* embarking is the best rule we can offer.

In short, learning styles are a significant cultural variable. Mostly, people who are task-oriented simply require enough information to get going. The major assumption for these people appears to be that they are only interested in a specific task. For example: if there's a task labeled A and found on page 6, the user will probably never look at a task labeled C or M.

Users in places other than North America may, very likely, want to read every word and really learn all there is to know about a given product before beginning to work with it.

Another common assumption is that the user reads the overview first. Not necessarily! Some people look at an index first, while others go to a table of contents

Linear Instructional Design, as typified by the standard flow chart, does not work well with the new technologies. This is because the new technologies are not that linear in the way information is organized for presentation and retrieval.

Non-linear tutorials and instructions must be arranged to conform to hypertext, Information Mapping, or web configuration. Using graphics can help with this issue.

Working with an instructional designer who has experience and interests in a non-linear design can result in more usable instruction which is better adapted to the newer technologies. One example of a non-linear design (with links disabled) can be found at: **www.ewinters.com/learningcontract.html.**

5 TECHNOLOGY AND INFRASTRUCTURE IN TARGET CULTURES

This Section lists some of the many considerations that fall under the general classification of environment. The relationship of people to their immediate environment, as well as to the planet as a whole, is culturally linked.

It is necessary to understand how colleagues, customers, and the end user identify with the concept of environment as you address these questions.

- Who is the user?
- Where are they physically?
- What is the equipment and infrastructure situation? For example, does each individual user have equipment, or is it shared?
- How will the information you are preparing be used? One manual shared among several users? Or one manual per individual?
- Is paper the appropriate medium?

These questions require serious consideration as decisions are being made. (These are ALL audience identification questions and ideally should be answered in an initial needs analysis.)

When equipment is shared, it may be a poor idea to put information online or on CD-ROM, as moving between media can be time-consuming and personally irritating. A hypertext organization might not be appropriate in such a context.

Paper or even a short video may be more practical. Consider cost. Ask yourself:

- Is physical space scarce?
- Will paper, CDs, or video be stored? How will they be stored?
- What are the preferences of the users?

Environmental Protection Issues

All the globally responsible issues might also be given serious consideration:

- Can you use recycled paper?
- Is soy ink possible?
- Are you recommending as many biodegradable products as possible?

Perhaps, most importantly, am I asking these questions in a culturally appropriate manner? You may be asking a question that has to do with unavailable or impossibly expensive resources. The answer might result in a loss of face.

6   CROSS-CULTURAL BUSINESS COMMUNICATION AND TECHNOLOGY

Effective communication between people, cultures and companies is based on relationships. Ideally we would personally meet and get to know each working-group team member, each distributor, each customer, and each vendor to create these relationships. Since this is not possible, in the majority of cases, we need to take advantage of all available tools to facilitate communication and relationship building.

Communication Tools, Applications, and the Web

The computer, Internet, and telephone are today's primary tools for cross-cultural communication. Global Corporations create secure intranets and maintain websites. Individuals do, of course, communicate via face-to-face meetings but they increasingly rely on emails, instant messaging, and discussion group postings. The telephone will continue to be a primary tool for communication as the conference call is a well-established institution. Increasingly those calls will travel over the Internet and contain video and multi-media components. Faxed communications are declining in number as electronic file sharing and the transmission of scanned documents as email attachments explode. Everyone searches globally for personal and business information via the computer portal to the Internet.

From these facilitated personal and business relationships come new products and services and the media campaigns to sell them.

There are many computer applications designed to assist in this work. Examples include, enhanced speech recognition, multilingual multimedia, language learning and translation, content management and online documentation, and customer support. For current information on these and other topics, consult MultiLingual News at **news@multilingual.com**.

When it comes to websites, content/information and interactive design are what drive "page views" or "hits." For an overview and evaluation of corporate websites, visit the Byte Level Research 2005 Web Globalization Report Card (**http://bytelevel.com/reports/global2005/**), a revised and expanded guide to the best and worst global websites. The Web Globalization Report Card rates 200 websites across 16 industries. In addition, the report profiles a number of websites in-depth, including Wal-Mart, Philips, Sony, BMW, GE, and the NFL. The Web Globalization Report Card is a valuable resource for companies seeking to upgrade their identities and position their products.

Language Learning and Translation Resources

The Internet presents language learning and translation resources that are easily revealed with a Google search. Finding quality resources among the offerings is the challenge. Here, networking with other users, joining a chat room regarding a specific product or service, and submitting a sample text for translation will help in your evaluation. From our experience, offers of language fluency in 12 days and "automated" online translations leave much to be desired. A free demo can be very revealing and offer an opportunity to explore a new application, service, or teaching methodology.

Interactive intranets and controlled-access online surveys are very popular vehicles for companies to disseminate information to, and get feedback from, worldwide operations. While these are not open to the public, they are numerous and important because they provide an opportunity to extend a corporate culture while respecting local languages and cultures among the "corporate family." They must be well crafted and should incorporate input from worldwide colleagues within the corporation.

Computers and Translation

Computer memory and the applications that enable machine translation are powerful resources for international cultural communicators. To be clear, there are programs that will translate a text from one language into another, and there are computer-based translation memory tools. These are called MT (machine translation) and TM (translation memory) tools.

Machine translation (MT) applies linguistic rules and a primary and secondary subject dictionary to a text. The source code (programming) driving these applications is very complex and very proprietary. Babel Fish, on the Internet from AltaVista, provides a good introduction to this type of tool.

Translation Memory

Translation memory (TM) is memory of previously translated text. TM tools will evaluate a single document for repeated words and phrases and will work within that document by creating a document-specific, bilingual memory as the human translator inputs the translation. TM tools also have the ability to consult vast database memories containing previous translations of other documents and suggest translation matches based on exact matches as well as based on fuzzy logic. So the more this tool is used, the more powerful its memory becomes. During translation, when the TM application "sees" a word or phrase similar to or the same as one previously translated, it automatically calls up the previous translation(s), which the translator can then accept, reject, or adjust appropriately and insert into the translation.

Translation memory contributes to consistency in translation terminology and to translation efficiency. The resulting lower translation costs should be a topic of discussion with your translation vendor.

Not all document translations can benefit from TM, but many can. In the final analysis it takes a skilled linguist/ translator to make the judgment calls regarding the use of text translations suggested by TM and to post-edit the text produced by MT. MT output without human post-editing is generally used only to identify key words in a document or to indicate the gist of the document contents. MT, at its current stage of development, cannot be relied on, by itself, for correct and complete translation from one language and culture into another language and culture.

Communication Tools In the Future

We live in a good time for communicators. The communication tools available today are increasingly affordable and accessible. As communication volume increases exponentially, the rewards will go to the adept. To succeed, we must become expert in the use of tools, provide superior content, and find creative ways of presentation.

7   Writing for Translation

Good news A well-written document with consistent terminology translates well into other languages. When creating a technical communication in English, it helps the translation process considerably if you can educate yourself in the use of Simplified English.

Simplified English

SE is controlled language and is characterized by its use of simplified grammar and style rules, and an established limited vocabulary with restricted meanings.

If you are not familiar with these simple techniques, here is a set of guidelines you may find useful:

- Include one thought or action per sentence.
- Use standard and consistent terminology.
- Create a list of all acronyms and technical terms, with definitions, for the translators. (This list contributes to the translation glossary, which is usually prepared before translation begins and really helps with the consistency requirements.)
- Provide conversions of all units of measurement, for example, feet to meters.
- Use active prose. Changes in verb tense and active/ passive voice seriously complicate the translation process.
- Use prepositions clearly.
- Use articles whenever possible

- Avoid over-modified nouns. It is frequently difficult to translate the concept when it is originally expressed this way.

Cross-cultural Humor

Writers sometimes add comic relief (for themselves) and encourage reader interest with a clever turn of a phrase or with humor. These devices are acceptable, but have meaning only within a specific cultural context. They frequently translate poorly, or not at all.

It is also possible to offend; what is terribly funny to you may be completely devoid of humor to a person from another culture. Or worse—it might be offensive. Avoid the use of idioms, slang, sports, and other culture-bound analogies for the same reasons.

Graphics for Translations

Use callouts (which layer on top of a graphic) rather than text embedded in the graphic. Doing so enables you to translate the callouts without having to edit the graphic.

Using "pre-organizers"—such as graphics, icons, numbered lists, and bulleted lists helps the user as well as the translator. Beforehand, determine if they are understandable, as well as acceptable, in the target culture.

Core Text

All product and user documentation is revised when products change. Always try to anticipate where in the text future changes will be documented. You can then create core sections of text that will be unaffected in future iterations. This reuse of core text considerably reduces the time and expense of future translations.

The translated text should be imported into your conventional publishing software file, if possible. This can best be done by over-writing your files. In this way the graphics and formatting can be maintained while the source text is replaced by the translation. Provide the translator with your electronic files to make this incorporation possible. This saves time and money. Your company's preferred publishing software should work well with all languages that use romanized alphabets.

Character Sets in Other Languages

Translations using Asian character sets, Arabic, or Hebrew may require a different operating system, software, or character-set. Confirm file and application compatibility before beginning a project and before you sign a purchase order. Ask the translator to send test files to the graphic designer, desk top publishing (DTP) technician, and/or to the print vendor. Non-roman character-based text saved as an EPS file can help. with any incompatibilities. EPS (Encapsulated PostScript) files are scalable graphic files that allow the incorporation of non-roman alphabet text into standard DTP applications. For more information, see **www.adobe.com/products/postscript/main.html**.

Increasingly the Unicode Standard (**www.unicode.org**) for encoding alphabets and character-based writing systems is being adopted and eases the "font problem" between platforms and operating systems.

The Translation Team

The translation team typically includes:
- You (the client)
- a project manager
- an instructional designer
- a translator
- an editor/verifier
- a graphic designer
- a print vendor

The professional requirements of each team member must be taken into consideration if the final product is to be of the highest quality.

Listen to your people.

The Translation Process

Translations from English into other languages and cultures will be most successful if you follow these steps which have been group into three phases—Preparation, Translation, and Prepress:

Preparation

1. Discuss the purpose, tone, target audience, and format of the final output of the communication with the translator and, when appropriate, the instructional designer.

2. Study the source document to be translated.

3. Identify and define special terminology to be tagged for the glossary with the help of a resource person, for example, an engineer or a programmer.

4. Ask the translator to identify difficult or unclear language in the source language. Discuss alternate expressions in the source language, as well as in the target language.

Translation

1. A native speaker of the target language with current knowledge of the target culture prepares a draft translation.

2. A second native speaker edits the draft translation.

3. The project manager discusses any comments with the translator and editor. Appropriate changes are incorporated.

4. The field editor or verifier designated by the client reviews and confirms the terminology and style of the translation.

5. The project manager reviews the client edits and, after discussion with the translator, the edits are incorporated.

6. The final version of the translation is returned to the same client editor/verifier for final approval.

Prepress

1. The translated text is input into the specified electronic publishing program.

2. Laser proofs of the document are sent to the graphic designer for final adjustments. Do not fax these proofs as distortions occur.

3. Your communication is produced to design standards and sent to the print vendor.

Translation is a team effort. It takes time and coordination. Short cutting these steps is not cost effective.

8 INTERNATIONALIZATION AND INTERNET COMMUNICATION

Increasingly, a product must be made available globally and must meet corporate needs in order to:

- extend areas of profitability
- accommodate customer requirements
- retain loyalty

Communicators, salespeople, and others, by paying close attention to customer and end user needs, can assist in these areas.

One definition of internationalization is the process of removing all cultural context from a program or document. This results in a more generic product to which one appends a list of culturally specific items that can be localized, depending on the target country. This facilitates the translation process and the creation of a localized document that looks and feels as though it was created in the target country or market.

Components that must be localized can include, but are not limited to:

- screens
- on-line help
- manuals
- registration cards
- licenses
- marketing collateral

- music
- art
- direct mail pieces
- promotional material

When writing for the Internet, which typically is email, newsgroups, and websites, you may fine these tips useful:

- Keep sentences and paragraphs as short as possible.
- Think concise rather than cryptic. White space on the screen greatly improves clarity.
- A blank line adds only one byte to the article length.
- Choose words carefully. Consider whether what you have written could be misinterpreted.
- As with other writing for translation or for an audience that may be using your language as a second or third language, avoid abbreviations and acronyms.
- Subtlety does not communicate well when written and may be lost on your audience.
- Most people reading your posting do not know you.

Humor can often be misinterpreted. Identify and clarify your humor with:

- smileys :-)
- frowns :-(
- winks ;-)

When answering email, we recommend that you:

- Have the original message fresh in your mind.

- Remember that when your answer is received, the original message may be lost with the passage of time.
- Do not include the entire message you are replying to. Reduce it to the absolute minimum needed to explain and give context to your reply.
- Use upper and lower case letters; they are easier to read.
- Leave in articles (such as: the, a, an). Deleting them can mangle the meaning of your sentences and take longer to read.

Remember that this is an international, global communication device. People all over the world are reading your words. Say it succinctly to have greater impact. The longer the posting, the sooner the reader gives up.

The subject line is there to enable a person with a limited amount of time to decide whether or not to read your comments. Tell people what the email is about before they read it. Some programs may truncate the length of the subject line to 40 characters, so keep your subjects short and to the point. Never say in ten words what you can say in fewer.

Once something is posted to the network, it is in the public domain. When you own the appropriate rights— you wrote it yourself—post it with a valid copyright notice.

Keep text in a generic format. Many people reading on the Internet do so from 80 column terminals or from workstations with 80 column terminal windows. Keep your lines of text to less than 80 characters for optimal readability.

Society and the Internet

Our immediate tendency is to see the Internet as a technology. It's really more a social phenomenon made possible by technology. It will continue to change along with other human institutions.

Those who have never tried electronic communication may not be aware of its necessary social skills. Think always that you are in a mixed cultural situation and behave accordingly.

Good manners are always appropriate.

World Wide Web communications

- Provide an email address, not merely a website or URL address (**http://www.*site address***).
- Include a human contact email, so visitors can obtain answers not provided by the web page.
- Include a short statement of what the web page is about; put it on the opening page.
- If you are a business, provide an internationally functioning phone and/or fax number.

As is the case with the clothing one wears or the atmosphere created in a room, a website reveals the personality of a person or institution.

We can read a web page and consider it:
- kind or thoughtless
- informative and helpful or self-serving
- clear or confused
- dynamic or dull

One reads the page and sees how well the designer understands the medium. Good, bad, or indifferent, on each screen we read information about the developer.

As with any other project, define the audience. The more specifically you can determine the needs of the people reading your website, the better you will meet those needs.

As with other forms of communication, do not assume how your website will be viewed, or by whom.

Localizing

Here is a *very* brief list of issues to consider when communicating your message to a global World Wide Web audience. Clearly, this list is a starting point; you will have your own considerations.

- What content management system does your website use? The basic architecture of content needs to be thoroughly examined. The architecture must be capable of managing updates across several languages. Consult with your system administrator *first*.
- Do you have sales, manufacturing, or personnel operations in countries outside your own country? Do you have contact information for them listed on the corporate website?
- Are you offering downloads of a product to your visitors and potential customers? Software, shareware, text files? Think about downloads as part of your localized content effort. A "Global Downloads" link can be valuable. Visitors from beyond North America will be appreciative.

- Localize images; pay attention to color and the icons and graphics associated with HTML coding. For example, when an icon says: "Products", consider localizing that icon for Spanish and have an icon that says, "Productos". Publishing localized text without translated graphics renders your message suspect in the mind of the reader or viewer.
- What are the top three accessed areas of your website? Press releases, company background, product descriptions? Consider localizing these frequently visited areas.

Additional localization suggestions:

- Would a FAQ (frequently asked questions) sheet per product be beneficial?
- Should you include corporate information on how your firm was founded?
- Do you provide opportunities for comments? Is the system localized for visitors who are not English speakers? Many non-English speakers access World Wide Web content daily. A localized comment system is one method. Emails can be forwarded to those who both understand and can respond to visitors in the language they have selected. Many different kinds of information can be incorporated into a localized opinion system
- Content is *the* superstar. People come to your site because they want easy access to information about you and what you offer. Provide a detailed site map and then add links to the localized content on your website. Your demonstrated commitment to their comfort level and

comprehension will have obvious beneficial results.

- Do you have a strong intellectual theft policy? Consider localizing this critical content. Theft occurs. A common justification by the thieves is that they did not know the material in question was proprietary. The thief may not understand English and, thus, not grasp the full meaning of your policy. When the policy is localized for languages in which your software is widely used and purchased, the language excuse is no longer convincing.

- Privacy is a serious matter. Assure visitors that personal information will never be sold to third parties, if this is true. The privacy statement should be prominently visible on the home page, and localized.

9   SELECTING AND MANAGING TRANSLATION RESOURCES

The goals of selecting and managing the translation process are to:

- produce materials of high communicative quality in a cost-effective manner
- be sensitive to the cultural expectations of the target audience
- plan for efficient revisions and updates
- produce the final product on schedule

Building Your Team

- Ask colleagues and professional contacts for recommendations regarding translation resources.
- Contact translators and translation companies.
- Ask to see samples of completed projects and ask for ten client references.
- Check the references by leaving a message after hours stating: "XYZ has named you as a reference. If they are exceptional and you would use their services again, please call me at 510-843-5600. Thank you." Keep track of how many replies you receive.
- Describe your project requirements in a memo, as clearly as possible.
- Loan an electronic copy of the source documentation to the translators, and solicit a written bid.

- Ask for the translation of a sample text you select. (You may or may not have to pay for this work.)
- Negotiate with your translator. This will give you insights into the style and quality of a translation of your documentation.
- Submit this test translation for review by your field editor or have another language professional judge its quality, and possibly ask for a *blind back translation* into the source language.

A blind back translation requires that the translated text be translated *back* to the source language. The back translator works without seeing the original text. By comparing the original source to the back translation, you can verify the completeness and accuracy of the original translation. This also provides an opportunity to resolve any issues arising from nuances and shifts in meaning between the two languages.

Supporting the Team for Success

Provide adequate time for project completion. Translation is all too frequently treated as the final and annoying obstacle to getting a product into the international marketplace.

A rushed translation increases the risk of inconsistent use of terminology and other mistakes. The larger the team of translators and the tighter the deadline, the greater the editing burden, including rewrites and additional costs.

Translation Glossaries

Search your company files for previous successful translations and glossaries for documentation. These can be helpful and instructive for translators and often can be incorporated into the current project. Ideally, source documents should be complete, finished (locked), and appropriate to the product version before being sent to the translation agency.

A translation glossary of terms is critical to success. This should be prepared and agreed to before the translation begins. Having a glossary contributes to the consistent use of terminology. This is especially true on larger projects when several translators will be working on the same document. The glossary can be added to, modified and used in future updates. Controlling the glossary allows for flexibility in choosing translators for future projects.

Your company participates in and pays for glossary creation. Retain full rights and access to the glossary during and after the project.

Translating Software Documentation

Software documentation is rarely finalized when the translation starts, so take extra care to keep track of versions. Ideally the documentation translation comes after the program or product has been localized. That way the screens appearing in the documentation are taken directly from the software and the correct version of the document is ensured.

Expectations, Deadlines, and Deliverables

Clear expectations, communication, and agreements contribute to the success of a project. The workflow and hand-off of deliverables must be agreed to in writing in advance.

Cost overruns and delays are usually the result of overtime or adding more translators to the project. This can be due to rush scheduling, client changes, increased word count, and delays in waiting for client edits and approvals.

Target document specifications include:
- defining the audience
- target country information
- cultural context

Editing and Verifying the Translation

Editing and verification by the client is critical to success and should match the production schedule. Ignoring this can cause last minute delays.

If an agency promises perfect translations and tells you no client review is necessary, be skeptical. Ask for the translation as it is produced and get it formatted in the agreed application. Have it checked. Do not wait until the "final delivery" to discover you have a problem.

For your peace of mind and to provide comments to the translators as soon as possible, have another language professional check quality. The verifier's scope of responsibility must be defined. Ideally, one verifier for each language combination should be in direct contact with the translators for the duration of the project to ensure consistency.

Should the verifier cover style and terminology? Translators typically prefer that the verifier comment only on word choice, as questions of style can cause great debate and delay. Fundamental questions of style should be resolved with an evaluation of the sample translation.

Identify the person with final editorial authority. Remember that mistakes should be corrected at no cost to you. Changes in the source text create changes in the translation. This increases project cost.

Who in the organization has authority to make changes and bear the financial responsibility?

Finally, understand your print vendor's requirements. Conduct compatibility tests by sending sample files and outputting them.

Before anything goes to print, your editor must approve the translation. Your designer must approve the laser proofs that show the exact document layout. Even small changes to layout can affect hyphenation.

Have your language professional give a final read for correct word breaks after the final design adjustments have been made. Changes, once translation begins, increase costs and cause delays.

The principles we have explored here are useful in any cross-cultural communication situation.

Bon Voyage!

Essays by Robert Sellin

An Ear for Language

Some people really do have an ear for language. Good for them. For those of us who do not, take heart.

We all know that speaking the language of another culture will open doors to opportunity and windows to new world views. Learning to speak another language takes motivation, dedication, and patience. Nevertheless, it is well worth the effort. Language skills facilitate new relationships, friendships, and adventures.

The good news is that we live in an era of optimal access to language learning resources. The choice to pursue them, or not, is ours. Many educational institutions offer opportunities to spend a year abroad and study language while immersed in another culture. Such an experience provides an invaluable foundation for lifetime learning.

Once we enter the working world, few of us are able to take the time to immerse ourselves in language learning by putting all things aside to study and live in another culture for months or years at a time. So consider a shorter "intensive" immersion opportunity of a week or two. There are programs specifically designed to combine vacation and language learning. Some programs are specifically designed for working people and may even cater to certain disciplines, to facilitate learning specialized vocabularies.

If an in-country learning opportunity is not available, investigate the classes and teachers in your own community. As with all things, the Internet offers a wealth of resources and is the place to connect with others sharing your interests. Many communities have evening adult school classes for language learning where a group setting can be fun and revive memories of your own school years.

With the advent of language courses on tape and CD, a significant portion of our commute time can be invested in language learning. Satellite radio brings foreign-language broadcasts into our cars and homes. Foreign language television is also available via satellite and cable. Most people are initially put off by these broadcasts because "they talk too fast." But with a little focus you will learn words and get a sense of a language's rhythm. As you learn more words you will hear them being used. Remember that what sounds fast to you is normal speech for the native speaker. Some people find it helpful to rent movies in another language.

Once you acquire basic language skills you can join a weekly conversation group or look for a conversation partner. I know a man who lives in Spokane, Washington who regularly meets with a Korean tutor, for example. In your home, with a pen and post-its, you can put names on all objects, remembering to include the article that denotes gender. This technique is very effective and "natural" as it associates the name directly with the object. This direct connection between object and name reduces translating from English. You can try to "think" in the other language as you begin your day or fall asleep at night.

Take heart in the knowledge that language learning helps keep your mind active and healthy. Observe the focus of the child who spends endless hours dedicated to language learning. While young minds do learn faster, you have the advantage of already having mastered one language. That language mastery can be your foundation and reference system of language sounds and rules. This can help in the intellectual understanding of a new language. Combine that understanding with a willingness to speak and speak again and again and again, and you will have the formula for success.

Once we start down the path of learning a new language, every lesson, every new word, every exchange of a greeting and each conversation will have a cumulative effect.

Cultural Curiosity

While traveling and conducting business across cultures, I am often reminded that our United States culture is quite young. The marketing of our young and brash culture across all media makes it fashionable and engaging to (most) other peoples. We have enjoyed business successes also with our unique "can do" style of brashness and technologically innovative products.

When brashness crosses the line to perceived arrogance, it becomes a real liability. It is always important to respect other cultures and to learn as much about them as possible. While we have our way of conducting business, other cultures do too. In fact, many cultures have well-developed and older business/barter systems, as compared with ours. Think about your own experiences to put this observation into perspective. Have you ever had the experience of a changed order—quantity or price—after the deal was signed? Have you bargained for a souvenir and after much effort realized you still paid too much?

The commercial world knows that we are a people in a hurry. When we are too impatient to complete a deal, we miss opportunities. Those who have more patience can use our hurried approach to their own advantage. Our potential customers know we want quick results. They usually know the date and time of our return flight to the U.S.A.. Don't be surprised if the real negotiating begins four hours before your flight departure time.

Building trust is an important part of business negotiation and it may be more difficult to develop across cultures. Building trust must be based on a genuine interest in your customer and an honest appraisal of your product offering and of yourself. Most foreign clients/buyers will be gracious, welcoming, and patient, to a point. That point of "this meeting is over" can arrive quickly if you are not perceived as a respectful and honest agent who is offering real value.

If our competitors have taken the time to develop relationships based on trust while we beat the drum of speed and price, it should not surprise us if we do not make the sale. Trust will frequently trump price alone. Remember that if you do obtain an order based on price-point alone, your future business is only as secure as your price. There will always be someone offering a lower price, even in this era of the declining U.S. dollar, and your customer will jump to a new supplier if price is the only consideration.

I believe that generosity and curiosity about others and their cultures is the foundation for a successful international business career. Pursuing that curiosity will lead to insight and understanding. As you develop better understanding of cultural norms and expectations, you will also develop respect for the culture with which you are dealing. After the initial courtesies are exchanged, it is mutual respect and acceptance that are the basis for developing real relationships. And relationships are the foundation for business success.

On Being Yourself

Have you ever participated in a business transaction with a compatriot who is "more Chinese than the Chinese"? Have you had a competitor who is more "Mexican than the Mexicans"? This is one way of reacting to another culture but it may not be the most successful way to function. How we react to other cultures is important and can be broadly grouped into three choices: reject, adopt, or adapt.

Rejecting another culture is an inappropriate way to do business in today's multicultural business environment. Those who believe that the American Way is the Only Way often use this approach. While American culture—as expressed in its films, music, and some of its commercial products—is known throughout the world, don't assume that other cultures embrace the American approach to negotiating business transactions. Indeed, such an attitude will be seen as a rejection of local cultures. It will contribute to stress and frustration for all concerned.

Adopting other cultures is another reaction. Adopting a different culture is trying to become a member of that culture, while disavowing your own culture. This attempt to "go native" can be entertaining for the locals but ultimately limits our ability to function in the culture. Like the old phrase "we are what we eat," we are inevitably a product of our upbringing and our experiences. It is counter productive to disavow our previous experiences because it limits our appreciation of ourselves and is perceived as artificial by members of the host culture.

Adapting is, in my experience, the healthiest response to another culture. When we adapt to another culture we recognize that we are functioning between cultures. We admit that we are members of our own culture and that we are also working in a very different culture. This honesty with one's self will feel comfortable and be appreciated by others.

I am reminded of an experience in Mooloolaba, Australia, a resort community north of Brisbane. Like many Australian beach communities, Mooloolaba has a Surf Life Saving Club on the edge of its magnificent sweeping beach. A sign outside the club admonishes that one must be either a member or a "bona fide guest" to enter the facilities and use the dining room, bar, and gaming room. Unaccustomed to the ways of Australia, I assumed that a bona fide guest must be a certified lifesaver, and searched my wallet for my Red Cross Life Saving Card. By doing so, I was applying assumptions that are a product of my own culture. When I attempted to present the same at the reception desk, I was greeted with a friendly laugh and the comment, "no worries Mate; with your accent, you're bona fide." I learned that, under Australian law, a bona fide guest is someone who lives at least 75 kilometers from the Club. That approach to club membership is completely inconsistent with the American experience. We quickly adapted to this new definition and were able to participate in a new cultural experience. We enjoyed some wonderful meals and conversation while dining in the club and overlooking the beach.

By adapting, you can function in both cultures. You will have experiences and enjoy opportunities that would not be available to you if you reject the other culture or if you deny your own.

ARTICLES BY ELAINE WINTERS

Across the Pacific Pond

This is a very personal view of Japanese, Chinese, and North American negotiating environments. There are horrific traps in discussions about cultural differences; stereotyping is the obvious, and major, one. *Stereotypes are used here to provoke thought and questions.*

What is negotiation? What do people actually do during a negotiation?

Negotiation, as an idea, is unique and culturally specific.

For North Americans, business dealings with many Asians, generally, are challenging to conduct and sometimes difficult to conclude satisfactorily. The obstacles are cultural in nature.

The Japanese tend to rely on generating solutions to problems from the information available, while North Americans use the idea of exchange (proposal-counterproposal). In addition, the Japanese emphasize the relationships involved as well as specified goals during negotiations. They really want to know who they are dealing with, who sent them, and what the future of this relationship might hold.

The criteria for determining how negotiators are selected differs in all cultures and includes such variables as professional status, hierarchical status, negotiating ability, knowledge of counterparts, and experience. In Asian communities, age can be an important factor.

How much do people rely on verbal or nonverbal signals to communicate their messages? More awareness of nonverbal signals means a highly complex society, that is high context in nature.

There is far more reliance on nonverbal signals for the Chinese and Japanese in acquiring information than for North Americans, generally.

Using Information

Even when North Americans know about a particular set of cultural differences, they do not know how to use the information. It can take some time before they find out.

There are two significant information lags: one is a genuine lack of information about the other culture— North Americans do not know very much about what goes on in Asian cultures. This is changing. However, it is changing slowly. The other is a 'what to do with the information now that we've got it' gap. Confusion exists due to a lack of real experience in working with people having different values, organizational styles, and negotiating strategies.

Stereotypes can result when assuming that any single person is going to reflect the group or even the group norm, which can lead to terrible misunderstandings. There is also the danger of viewing a culture as a static entity instead of an evolving, fluid, environmentally oriented organism.

Successfully Negotiating the Process

One critical component to a successful negotiation is agreeing to the process of *how* the parties will participate. Both sides must recognize the other side as part of the process. Each side cannot always assume equality in attitude.

The other is responsiveness. What you as a negotiator do, should, in some observable way, be responsive to the needs of the other side.

There should be mutual movement—both sides must move from their original positions over the duration of the negotiation. This cannot be assumed either. Not every culture regards this as effective negotiation; it may be seen as loss of face, for example.

A Chinese negotiator can be a bit vague about their personal role or position and their specific responsibilities in any given situation. They appear, to the North American sensibility, to be 'manipulative', using conflicting feelings, including friendship, obligation, guilt, and something resembling dependence. The overt appearance is that they are trying to shame North Americans into making concessions.

The Chinese often present a face that on the surface will not take risks, seems evasive, uses what appears to be delaying tactics, and uses the claim of 'ignorance' as a vehicle for gaining information.

Frequently, they let it be known that they are negotiating with your competition and, most irritating of all to North Americans, sign contracts, and then do not exhibit any behavior to indicate they are bound by such an agreement.

They send more negotiators to bargaining sessions than North Americans tend to do, leaving said Americans to feel outnumbered as well as somewhat out-foxed.

The Japanese are frequently perceived as pressing for additional information with no corresponding offering gestures.

They are very slow to make concessions (giving too little, and waiting too long to do it). It is difficult to get them to reveal who the pivotal person is in the negotiation. They are also charged with being 'inscrutable', and using 'confusing' tactics when communicating.

So, a brief summary of these differences: North Americans feel that both the Chinese and Japanese:

- are deliberately difficult negotiators
- are not really sincere about wanting to come to agreements
- ask for information without offering anything in return
- push for concessions and never reciprocate as much or as often as North Americans expect

Solving the 'Difference' Problem

A broad range of possible actions include culturally responsive or sensitive strategies.

I would like to suggest *five* possible *individual approaches* and *three* strategies that are a *combinations of ideas* that can be implemented during negotiation. Although the focus here is on two Asian countries— China and Japan—perceived from a North American perspective, these broad suggestions may be usefully applied to a country, regional, or even an organizational culture.

Individual Options and Strategies

1. Use your own culture's approach. To be successful, it will be necessary to convince the other side to use your culture's ways. (This option is used very

infrequently. It is perceived as totally arrogant and, therefore, not productive.)

2. Use the others party's ways to negotiate. Embrace their way of doing things. Difficult, at best.

3. One party modifies their method. This lies between the first two. Adapting some of your methods brings you closer to the other's way of doing things. Workable, and not very easy.

The following two concepts tend to change the strategies of the parties involved or change the process itself.

4. Find an advisor who knows the other culture very well and makes suggestions; like an agent who will negotiate for you. In some cultures referred to as a 'talking chief.'

5. Introduce a new way—something not typical of either culture involved—something entirely divergent. Personalize negotiation methods and approaches.

Do not ignore culture (impossible anyway!). Try to treat it as background. Focus on the capabilities of the specific individuals at the table. This approach is frequently successful because a new, mutually agreed upon culture is being created just for this effort.

Common Options and Tactics

Three shared strategies are listed below. I call them 'shared' because they require very specific coordination and agreement with an individual counterpart.

1. Use a mediator—an intermediary both sides agree on—who can moderate the discussions. This can be useful and productive when the 'right' person is

found. They must be someone who can remain 'neutral.'

2. Coordinated adjustment. This approach applies in situations where a strategy is explicitly addressed and the sides decide to use some aspect from each culture. This is a shared version of adapting.

3. A personalized procedure that transcends cultures. In collaboration, the negotiator puts culture in the background and concentrates on the particular individuals involved. For example, a third culture is accessed or a special subculture created to carry out negotiations effectively—a virtual culture.

In selecting a scheme, consider feasibility. Some strategies involve a high degree of knowledge of the other culture. Consider your level of knowledge as well as your counterpart's knowledge of your culture.

Additional Considerations

Consider the unique relationship you have with your counterpart.

Do you have a history? Long/short term? Have you negotiated with each other before? Recently? If so, how? Were the results successful?

Consider your counterpart's values, inclination, and probable strategy. What is this person likely to do?

Think realistically about their capabilities, including:
- truly readily available staff
- actual financial resources
- genuinely useable networks
- professional and personal contacts

Consider your own values and capabilities, as listed above. What actions are you willing to give up and/or embrace?

Implementation of any responsive, successful plan requires an ongoing respect for the counterpart's culture and a sensitivity to comments. Monitor all comments. If the strategy chosen is seen as not working, modify it or change the arrangement.

Relationship Building

The only way to successfully approach cross-cultural negotiations is to understand that you must develop a relationship with the other side. This enables an outcome inclusive to both sides.

The single most important factor in communicating with Chinese and Japanese people is acknowledging the difference in our cultural contexts: our low-context culture versus their high-context culture.

North Americans rely on conveying meaning through actual words. The Chinese and Japanese convey much of their meaning by what is not overtly said and by saying things subtly—relying a great deal on the context of how the information is delivered and by who—to supply meaning.

Presenting Information

When presenting information in your native language with fluent counterparts:

- Use firmness selectively and only when necessary.
- Refer to the relationship, as opposed to oneself.

- Be *very* sensitive to your nonverbal signals and how they are received.
- Be *completely* consistent across channels and media.

In presenting in your native language with non-fluent speakers:

- Use an interpreter agreed to by both parties.
- If not understood, *never* speak louder or repeat the same words.
- Explain information in more than one way. Use agreed upon images.
- *Always* avoid jargon and idioms.

When presenting in a non-fluent second language:

- Do not translate word for word. Communicate ideas and concepts!
- Use the foreign words and grammar you do know resourcefully—frequently, there's more than one way to get the meaning conveyed.
- Beware of 'false matches' between languages—words whose similar appearance (spelling) leads to the thought that the meanings are a match.

When presenting via interpreters:

- Request simultaneous or consecutive translation, as you see fit.
- Speak slowly, with frequent pauses.
- Employ your own or a mutually agreed upon interpreter.

Listening Tips

In discussions with the Chinese and Japanese:

- *Always* display respect toward your counterpart's views.
- The statements and actions you actually hear and see may be very different from your initial interpretations and assumptions.
- Consider intended as well as literal information.
- Recognize the counterpart's high communicative context; watch for nonverbal cues and messages contained in the context.
- Remember the interpreters may have limitations.

Summary

There are two major reactions North Americans (NA) seem to have when working with and negotiating with the Chinese and Japanese:

1. We (the NAs) are inexpert and clumsy.

2. We are being 'taken'; the process is unfair.

Three ideas to balance those reactions may prove useful:

1. There is no substitute for cultural knowledge of your own culture and counterparts.

2. Pursue goals consistent with the cultural context in which you both find yourselves.

3. Recognize the possibilities of options when selecting a strategy and, when possible, list them for all parties to consider.

Good luck and Bon Voyage.

Cultural Issues in Business Communication

Communication is more than just speaking, writing, and editing. It also involves information gathering and teamwork.

In the economy of the 21st century, this means communicating cross-culturally. There are three main components to any communication:

- subject matter
- medium of delivery
- cultural considerations

Of the three, the third is generally ignored. While fashionable phrases get uttered—mostly, celebrating cultural diversity—what results are mostly exercises in politically correct language or attempts at controlling personal irritation. Few people seem to feel the need to truly face the underlying issues that cloud even the simplest of delicate, and frequently confusing, cross-cultural interactions.

Icebergs

Culture? People have talked the idea to death. For our purposes lets define culture as the way in which each of us is programmed to behave in the environment.

Cultures are like icebergs—some features are apparent to anyone not in a fog, while others are deeply hidden. Above-the-surface features include overt behaviors, such as the ways people:

- dress
- eat
- walk

- talk
- relate to one another
- conduct themselves during public ceremonies such as weddings or funerals

Also included are things such as social distance. Other aspects of culture are so far below the surface that they are hard to recognize.

We may see evidence of these hidden aspects, but we usually cannot pinpoint them precisely and usually do not have a clue where they came from. They are hard to define even for our own culture because we take them in with our mother language. They might include:

- how we encode and retrieve information
- our concept of justice
- our perception of music
- proper parenting
- beauty or ugliness
- the meaning attached to 'teaching' stories
- what well-educated means
- what constitutes status

Convergence and Divergence

Global communication, transportation, and changes in living styles have begun to blur many of the surface distinctions between different cultures. Many cultures are adopting Western dress, for example.

The deeper differences remain. For example, compare the respect due to elders in some Asian and African societies—still true today even in modern urban environments—with the way seniors are viewed in many Western countries.

While there is some surface convergence, there is divergence as well. In fact, the world seems to become more tribal as opportunities for communication expand.

For example, as the idea of a unified Europe becomes a reality, many people are exerting their differences more, not less. Alternatively, witness the ethnic strife and new nation-states that have emerged with the dissolution of the Soviet Union.

Cross-cultural communication is more important now than ever. How can this idea be put to practical use?

High- and Low-context Cultures in a Business Context

One of the deep or hidden aspects that differentiate cultures is the amount of context a culture's members expect in social interactions.

People who study such things divide cultures into those which are high context and those which are low context.

In general, high-context cultures place great importance on:

- ambience
- decorum
- the relative status of the participants in any given communication or a meeting
- the manner of a message's delivery—memo, speech, fax, video conference

Low-context cultures tend to want to ignore such things and emphasize the **content** of a communication, an attitude that might be expressed in the phrase "cut to the chase."

One example:

> Imagine a typical global business environment. Several team members have been gathered from around the world to attend a corporate meeting.
>
> At this meeting, they are expected to make essential decisions affecting corporate goals and objectives. Included on the new team are people from:
>
> - Korea
> - Malaysia
> - Singapore
> - South Africa
> - Germany
> - Denmark
> - Canada
>
> This is the first full face-to-face meeting of the entire team. They are all gathered in the foyer outside the conference room of the Seoul office.
>
> Formal introductions are made during this preliminary meeting while the team members breakfast on coffee, tea, and pastries.
>
> After a while, they all move into the conference room. The tables and chairs are arranged facing the front of the room in traditional classroom style.
>
> The Canadians, the Germans, and the Danes look rather unhappy and, with a few

disapproving words about this making for poor interaction, begin rearranging the furniture. The host Koreans look confused and make no comments.

The meeting begins. The agenda is announced. Issues are raised, discussed, and decided upon.

At the end of the morning session, the Germans comment to the Danes that the Koreans and Malays have not said much. The Canadians and the Danes nod in agreement, and shrug.

After lunch, the Korean host and a Malay colleague take the Canadian team leader aside and express very strong reservations about one of the decisions.

The Canadian is aghast; the morning meeting has been wasted; the discussion will have to begin again. "Why didn't you say so during the meeting?" he fairly shouts.

What Happened?

For the Asians, members of high-context societies, issues, circumstances, and relationships are **as** important as the work itself.

In this case, what is important is the business being discussed at the meeting. Interpersonal relationships were not developed well enough in this fledgling team to publicly raise the objection to an argument.

In addition, team members with higher status in the organization were present. The Asians' cultural orientation insisted that comments be made at a more private (appropriate) time. The context of where and how comments and opinions were heard was almost more important to them than the comments themselves. The others, coming from low-context cultures just wanted to get the job done.

The furniture was rearranged because the westerners were interested in the task and in getting it accomplished as efficiently as possible.

The Asians wanted to spend some time learning about each other and establishing a foundation for relationships. The classroom atmosphere and the brief opportunities for socialization were, in fact, exactly what they needed in this new organizational setting.

A Very Expensive Mistake

The *per diem* cost of gathering people from all over the world could easily reach tens of thousands of U.S. dollars.

The best that can be hoped for in this kind of a multicultural team situation is an environment that fosters the building of a shared culture: a context, mutually agreed upon wherein this "virtual" culture can grow, thrive, and benefit from the cultural richness of individual members.

The Challenge

So, let's take a look at this: people, programmed differently and with little or, at best, a superficial knowledge of each other, now have to communicate something in such a way as to make meaning clear and not provoke misunderstanding.

The message might be anything from a simple sales pitch ("buy my widgets") to an attempt by a global corporate leader to communicate a vision to employees in fifty countries. The communicator wants a particular and sometimes well defined reaction to the message.

The challenge is to get the desired reaction from the communication.

It is sometimes very difficult to do so.

Building Understanding

Understand the cultures you are attempting to communicate with. Begin by looking for rich points such as those found in a culture's rituals. Rich points provide a web of associations. By analogy, they may give you insights into the culture.

What does this mean?

Reading rich points is similar to learning a new language. For example, you're traveling and you notice such things as food, articles of clothing, etc., that are different, yet similar to things in your own culture. Your language skills say: replace this old word with this new one. (A *serape* is a blanket that is worn like a coat.)

Eventually you acquire a simple vocabulary in the new language. Similarly, you are somewhat familiar with various rites and rituals—weddings, funerals, rites of passage—that occur in every culture. Your cultural skills say: replace this idea with that one.

Eventually, you begin to understand, superficially and overtly, the new cultural environment. A web of understanding begins to develop based on prior experiences.

Sometimes, the language and cultural cues are such that you have no experience with the situation or any clues at all. It is nearly impossible to develop a 'web' in such a situation. At such times, you need a cultural guide— someone to provide you with the clues you will need to develop understanding.

Common Denominators

Know your audience well enough to be able to anticipate their reaction to your communication.

It is impossible to learn all the cultures you must communicate with, especially if you are developing something for export to many countries. The best you can do is try to find a common denominator and work from there.

Success Story

One successful example is the Macintosh Graphical User Interface with its folders and trash cans. Its use of icons and simple concepts satisfies the communication needs of most people. (Have you known anyone who experienced serious difficulty figuring it out on a MAC?)

Some people are such sophisticated users that the loss of total control over the details of the system irritates them. Others are confused by the icons on the screen and need additional help. Mostly, however, people looking at the interface can intuit what to do. This works regardless of language.

The lesson: giving most of your audience access to your material is not really impossible. However, doing so takes creativity and imagination.

Conclusion

Remember, above all: reality is *only an opinion*—yours and everyone else's. Your special reality is formed in the cultural environment in which you were born, raised, and spent most of your life. Your reality will never completely match someone else's.

Find commonality and work from there. Look for rich points and try to understand and use them. Create webs of insight and understanding.

With hard work and luck, you will find common denominators and achieve a high degree of mutuality in your cross-cultural communications.

Design Considerations for a Global Economy

-- stop worrying and do something to change the world

To successfully prepare communication material for an audience that may come from anywhere in the entire world, it is becoming increasingly necessary to educate ourselves about how people learn in different cultures.

Educating ourselves about other people means a lot more than how to order the appropriate dish in a restaurant when entertaining or being entertained. It means that we, as designers, writers, communicators, understand the rules of how information is acquired, processed, and retained for a particular group.

Evidence already exists for successfully integrating culture into language learning (Light, 1984; Feguson, 1984; Papalia, 1984). How can instructional design models bend and reshape to meet current corporate/ educational necessities?

Is including cultural constructs when working with the reality of multi-cultural audiences at home and abroad another meaning of honoring our several cultures (Doyle, 1990)?

There are similarities between acquiring a skill and learning a language. For example, ordering in a restaurant is a frequent and successful way to encourage students to articulate (produce) the target language. The individuals and events that must be taken into consideration in a restaurant setting are:

- roles (chef, server, bartender, cashier)
- interacting (or not interacting) with each of these people

- etiquette of ordering
- getting attention for service
- paying the bill

Learners are walked through these encounters and alternative language for a given situation is supplied. Practice ensues. The move from novice to master is at an individually determined pace.

How can we integrate a broad spectrum of presentation possibilities as well as content into the design of teaching how to use a new telephone system, how to use a new computer system, how to park your car, or a laboratory procedure? Is the same material usable in another, perhaps non-Western context? Does this idea apply to our increasingly diverse learning population?

Integration Process

Can we examine the task of integration as a series of steps? Here are some steps built on thoughts by several writers in the field (Bloom, 1956; Gagne, 1970).

Step 1

First, there are rituals (or heroes) of an identifiable group.

We usually see this in exercises with children in school. It manifests itself as celebrations and recognition of heroes and holidays. The most common examples you will be familiar with are Black History month and Chinese New Year (which is actually Lunar New Year, since it is celebrated in many countries—some of them Asian—and not just by people of Chinese origin!).

I think this level of information is probably satisfactory for young children. It tends to instill some familiarity with several cultures and acknowledge that different groups celebrate different things in different ways.

Children who come from a variety of backgrounds get a bit of recognition for their cultural group; parents feel that their ethnic heritage is being publicly acknowledged. The richness of the community is also celebrated.

Step 2

The second step adds to the first by honoring specific examples of individual contributions.

These are frequently tied to artistic accomplishments in literature, visual arts (such as films and video) and ideas (for example, philosophy).

Unfortunately, this can sometimes lead to training manuals and programs called, for example, "How To Manage Your East-Indian, Italian, Irish, East-European, or Asian Employees." It can also tend to stereotype ethnic characterizations, for example, attitudes toward time and space, behaviors, such as eating habits, and beliefs, such as religion or superstitions.

It does not have to be this way. Material exists which sheds light and insight (Secundy, 1991).

Step 3

The third step moves us on to a new and different plateau: how to understand problem solving within the cultural boundaries and norms of another culture (Hofstede, 1991; Finkelstein & Tobin, 1991).

Here are exercises and experiences in which events are viewed from the perspective of another culture. Examples abound. The two best known are described on the next page.

- Jane Elliot's blue eyes/brown eyes experiment[1]. (My first exposure to this kind of event was in the Peace Corps when our group played Bafa Bafa[2].)
- Barnga, a card game in which the rules change frequently (Thiagarajan & Steinwachs, 1990).

The participants learn a lot about themselves and how they view and respond to differentness, and how to characterize these experiences.

I have always valued this step as the time or the turning point, if you prefer, when an individual really finds out whether or not they truly respect another point of view and whether or not they can understand "walking in someone else's shoes."

Step 4

The fourth step builds directly on the third. Once another person's point of view is respected and understood, then it is possible to comprehend and act on that particular perspective.

An outgrowth of this is coming to agreement by consensus. In this process, every point of view is given

---

1. Blue eyes/brown eyes is the way Jane Elliot divided her 3rd grade class. Blue-eyed children were afforded many privileges; brown-eyed children were not, and were treated as inferior.
2. Bafa Bafa is a game in which participants adopt the behavior and values of functional societies.

equal weight. The discussion of each point is complete to the satisfaction of each participant.

All this is interesting, but what does it have to do with helping someone learn a new telephone system, computer system, or a laboratory procedure?

Lots.

For example, if you are working with a new software product and know it will be exported for sale, these events occur as the software is developed:

- The graphics expert lays out screen and menu templates.
- The translator raises issues of field sizes for other alphabets.
- The documentation people begin to write manuals.
- The instructional designer specifies objectives (when there is a tutorial).

You need to ask a few basic questions, such as:

What are the unique rules for information organization and learning for students from the culture or region where the product will be marketed and are these rules being considered (Hofstede, 1991)?

What are the cultural considerations in terms of:

- student
- employee
- instructor
- evaluation
- incentives
- individual responsibility
- group/individual activities

- group/individual recognition
- authority
- subordination

Will the learners have their instructional and/or, information transfer expectations met (Beire, 1984)?

Simple translations are usually inadequate. Material should be reorganized and realigned to meet different instructional needs for different world views and learning styles. This is not always possible in the *rush to market* world.

For example, if a significant portion of the audience experienced their early learning in a high-context environment, you will meet communication objectives more easily by:

- using more pictures
- breaking down task explanations into small pieces

Since producing different versions of the materials for different audiences is not practical, I suggest developing supplemental materials with extra explanations in additional handouts for those who want them. Perhaps a short videotape with additional information about a complex process might be included.

These adaptations or supplements need not be expensive and, in the long term, they *are* cost effective because the learners will not need to be retrained. People do not feel alienated or angry. They get it the first time around. They are successful.

Supplemental materials are also a good marketing tool, and a sales feature.

Can this attitude in instructional design develop into an approach wherein everyone is accommodated relative to their skills, talents, and learning styles?

Will this lead to worldwide nirvana, where social actions and national behavior are determined by a global perspective?

Will performance technologists reach their ultimate goal of providing truly appropriate interventions?

Only time can tell. The emphasis on considering differentness can only accelerate this change.

References

Beire, J. (1984). Questioning is different for each cultural group. Proceedings of SUNY Conference. Albany, NY, ED 262 577.

Bloom, B.S. (Ed) (1956). Taxonomy of Educational Objectives--The classification of educational goals--Handbook 1: Cognitive Domain. New York: David Mackay Co.

Doyle, R.H. (1990). Cross cultural competence is a requirement in business environments. Monograph, State University of New York. Plattsburgh, NY, ED 339 188.

Ferguson, H. (1984). Understanding bridges cultures. Proceedings of SUNY Conference. Albany, NY, ED 262575.

Finkelstein, B. & Tobin, J. (Eds.) (1991). Transcending stereotypes. Yarmouth, ME: Intercultural Press.

Gagne, R.M. (1996). The conditions of learning. New York: Holt, Rhinehart, and Winston.

Hofstede, G., (1991). *Cultures and organizations*. New York: McGraw-Hill.

Light, R. (1984). Communicative proficiency and cross-cultural issues. Proceedings of SUNY Conference. Albany, NY, ED 262 577

Papalia, A. (1984). Integrate culture. Proceedings of SUNY Conference. Albany, NY, ED 262 577

Secundy, M.G., Ed (1991). Trials, tribulations, and celebrations. Yarmouth, ME: Intercultural Press.

Thiagarajan, S., & Steinwachs, B. (1990). Barnga.Yarmouth, ME: Intercultural Press.

Preparing Material for Use by the Entire World

Let 'em eat cake, speak English, and think as I do.

Are you currently responsible for preparing print, interactive electronic, or visual materials for a client base that is marketing, selling, informing, or teaching to other parts of the world?

If that doesn't describe you at this moment in time, it will most likely be part of your job description in the very near future. That statement applies to everyone in a global economy. This is an equal opportunity challenge.

It is becoming increasingly necessary for those who are responsible for the transmission and interpretation of information to educate themselves about learners in different cultures.

As you already understand, educating ourselves about other people means a lot more than knowing how to order the appropriate dish in a restaurant when entertaining clients from out of town.

It means that as communicators of information, whether in print, electronically, or with pictures, we must understand the rules of how information is acquired, processed, and retained in a particular society.

When our responsibilities also include teaching or training, we must also understand pedagogical strategies and how they can be used advantageously in communication. In short, we must know how to engage intellectually, rather than present information that is passively viewed. (Both print and electronic tutorials can be viewed as providing information in a passive presentational way.)

It is also useful to understand the unique organizing principles of any particular group. What are the appropriate and accepted behaviors for those in various roles: student, employee, or instructor?

North Americans, for example, are very concerned with **content**; learners from another region may be more concerned with the **context** in which the information is presented.

If you go to a restaurant with colleagues, you may experience a lot of discussion about where to sit (and sometimes how to sit), what foods to try, how they are prepared, the ingredients, what to drink with what dish, and so on. The following behavioral factors are taken into consideration in a restaurant:

- roles (maitre d', chef, food server, bartender, cashier, customer, guest, host)
- degree of interaction, or non-interaction, with each of these people
- ordering etiquette (who's first, or does one person order for all?)
- eating etiquette (table manners)
- paying the bill etiquette (where and when)
- tipping etiquette (on the table, or presented to the waiter)
- ritual of leaving

The rules are different and distinct for each place.

I don't know about your experience. I have never found two French restaurants to be alike, either in North America, or in Paris, Lyon, or Nice. It is equally true for restaurants serving Thai, or Cuban, or Burmese, or

Mexican food. The varieties of examples in American society are ample.

Acquiring food at any baseball game is quite different from ordering in any elegant, and expensive, French restaurant.

When you are the stranger and you ignore the advice of colleagues and violate the rules in a restaurant, you're embarrassed and, perhaps, your colleagues are as well. Face can be lost. You may have demonstrated a serious lack of respect.

If you violate the rules during preliminary business discussions, or on a follow-up sales call, or with your marketing materials, you may lose your customer.

And again, face is lost.

If you violate the rules of organizing information when preparing materials for communicative purposes, you will not meet your objectives. You will have frustrated and unhappy clients and users. You have shown disrespect for the customer/student/participant.

In general, when preparing materials, you will need to develop a much greater level of detail for regions other than North America.

Very simply stated: High-density cultures[3] (for example, Japan, Turkey, and Peru) expect a greater level of detail in all interactions when compared with low-density cultures (for example, U.S.A., U.K., Austria). Think for a moment now and when tea is served in these cultures. What is the place of tea in British culture?

---

3. Meaning is derived from the delivery context. A high level of detail is expected in the verbal communication.

We know it is generally true that learning anything is usually more successful when the materials are situational.

If you've ever struggled to learn another language, you probably remember a few things to say at specific times—morning greetings, bidding farewell, asking for directions, and, our earlier example, surviving in a restaurant.

To ensure success, these situational materials always follow the organization rules for learning in that society.

Using the computer medium as an example, here are some specific things to consider as materials are prepared for an audience that is different, in terms of information organization, from one you may be accustomed to:

In the paper documentation (and this may also include handouts or workbooks being prepared for another context, such as a workshop), before the 'getting started' section, do the materials consider the larger context of the user's environment? In other words, is it important for the user in this unique culture, country, or region to have in-depth background on how the software was developed and by whom? (This does not mean three lines on the opening screen, or two sentences in the documentation introduction!)

As the software (or tutorial) is developed, the screens are designed, issues of field sizes for other alphabets are raised, documentation is begun, and the lesson plans for tutorials and online help is begun, here are a few questions for you to ask:

- What are the unique rules of learning for students, or participants, or manual users, or online help users, from that country, culture, or region?

- What are the presentation expectations? Are they being seriously considered and taken into account?
- Has that metaphor been completely researched. That is, will it intellectually work, make sense, and have the desired cognitive connection?

Translation, even when totally accurate, can be inadequate. Material should be reorganized and realigned to meet different learning rules for different world views and learning styles.

Strategies are readily available for successfully accomplishing these adaptations and, with planning from the outset, expenses can be kept to a minimum.

For example, it may be possible, and totally appropriate, to provide supplemental print or disk material instead of a complete second or third version for an individual region.

Americans think it best when our communication is explicit and direct. Others may expect information to come implicitly, in an indirect way.

Consider using many more drawings, diagrams, or other pictorial/graphic information when preparing for a culturally high-context audience.

If you're communicating something that is concerned with the notion of time, find out how that notion is perceived in the target culture.

American society, among others, perceives time as linear, and critical, and is rather exact about it.

Another society may think of time as elastic, and not terribly important, relative to other things.

The audience may come from, or have received education in, a part of the world that is "high context" in terms of organizing information. Alternatively, the learning environment at home may have been "high context." [4]

A short video may be enough to do the job. In that case, the body language, visible clues to interpersonal relationships, gestures of respect, and other culturally specific variables must be appropriate for the culture and the situation.

It will take more than a well-written manual or a software program (that really does meet a need) or slick packaging to accomplish effective information transfer or instruction in the global economy.

No matter where you live, you can prepare yourself in the following ways to meet these challenges:

- Volunteer in educational exchange programs.
- Host a student for a semester.
- Build a relationship with a peer from a different culture.
- Host a foreign visitor for a day or longer.
- Have a teaching or learning experience in a different cultural setting.
- Read children's stories or folklore from another society.
- Engage in travel and study another language.
- Most importantly, if your circumstances permit and you can arrange to do so, sojourn in another

---

4. High- and low-context cultures are explained in Section 1 on page 1

culture rather than simply being a visitor for a brief time.

You will learn a lot about yourself.

Tune in, find out, *listen*. Not everyone eats cake, speaks English, or thinks as you do.

Bon voyage!

New Technologies, Education, and the Developing World

Evolving technologies will play a pivotal role in the liberation of formal education from the constraints of geography, time, and human resources.

Such technologies present an opportunity to businesses and other organizations to aid in both teaching, learning, and working with institutional agents of change to transform the structure—and philosophy—of both educational systems and society itself.

In the developing world, education has been criticized for its inability to provide children with a system that ensures accessibility, quality, equity, and effective management. The colonial legacies of many developing countries have left them with introduced systems of education that are not meeting the needs of large segments of their populations.

Children living in urban poverty, or in poor rural environments, cannot afford to go to school in the standard 9:00a.m. - 3:00 p.m. time slot (frequently, they must work during that time period).

Even when schools are tuition free, the opportunity of going to school is denied to those boys and girls who are needed to perform chores at home, be responsible for younger siblings, work in the fields, or in an urban factory. Traditional barriers in some countries prevent young girls from leaving home after a certain age or studying in coed classrooms. Secondary schools or universities may be difficult for students to access geographically.

Quality is an issue; many education systems suffer from a shortage of adequately trained teachers, learning materials, and textbooks. In terms of equity, disparities clearly exist. The education given to different classes, races, gender, may be inferior to that provided the children of the ruling/educated/wealthy class.

Finally, many education systems suffer from ineffective management because administrators and planners lack current information and adequate tools with which to make appropriate decisions.

As global corporations seek a better educated work force, these issues can handicap a developing country.

The new technologies can serve as catalysts for deconstructing the introduced formalized nature of education systems and evolving more appropriate education systems in developing countries. The technologies can add new flexibility to the whole process, which results in broadened access.

Radio, television, and computer instruction are not bound by strict time schedules or geographic barriers. These technologies, and those that are evolving, can be used to complement lessons given by teachers; they can supplement what is frequently a crisis in shortages of skilled, trained, teachers as well as traditional printed material.

Reducing educational disparities has a lasting social benefit. Technology helps to level the playing field, by providing access to knowledge that has traditionally only been accessible to an elite population.

Given the various crises confronting the world, as well as the need developing countries have to improve their economic futures, we simply don't have a single person to waste.

On a micro level, technology is a tool for empowering individual learners and teachers. People learn in different ways. Technology offers the flexibility to accommodate different learning styles and abilities. This can be especially important in developing countries where large student-teacher ratios and a lecture style of teaching make one-on-one contact rare, and difficult.

Technology can be used to encourage creativity, collaboration, and communication, providing a means of communicating with peers beyond the confines of a local community.

This power to expose individuals to different ideas and people with whom they never would have the opportunity to interact, may be the greatest long term global advantage to the use of evolving technologies in education.

As the price/performance ratios of technology continue to improve (along with maintenance and technical support), the prospect of using these technologies to bring about large scale change becomes more and more a serious reality.

Despite all of these potential benefits, technology is not the panacea to either the developed—or the developing country's—problems with education. This is because technology is still controlled by human beings who are driven by their own political, economic, social, and cultural agendas. Nevertheless, useful content presented in a culturally appropriate way will find an audience.

A help for bureaucracy: through the use of management information systems, administrators and planners compiling and analyzing crucial data provide an opportunity for making better decisions concerning budgets, purchases, and school organization.

Technology involves thinking about appropriate applications, introducing new sources of information, and redefining the role of the traditional input entities such as teachers and textbooks.

Technology can help us work smarter. This develops a better educated workforce, improves business advantages. and goes a long way toward realizing commercial opportunities.

LETTERS FROM ELAINE WINTERS

Baklava 101

Well, I thought I knew about Baklava—and you probably think you do too. Fugetaboutit!

It comes in every shape you can imagine—with every kind of nut—paste/chopped and then drenched with every flavor of honey you can envisage. And probably a few you haven't. The filo dough is also flavored.

There is a shop that sells nothing else—steps from my hotel—(no apartment yet)—and I must pass it at least twice a day. What can I say?!

Istanbul is my kind of town—truly great food, every kind of music imaginable fills the air (acid rock, jazz, Beethoven), and both modern and traditional art is ubiquitous; people!—many look like they are on their way to a casting call for a Fellini movie.

The city itself is as huge and sprawling as LA or Shanghai or Mexico City—13 million people live here straddling Asia and Europe. It's crowded. Nobody can give you an exact head count because the census hasn't been taken 'in quite some time'—and I have no idea what that means. Thirteen million seems to be the generally accepted educated guess.

People arrive everyday from the countryside—for the reason people move to big cities everywhere. Unemployment in Istanbul is very high – it fluctuates between 15 and 20 percent from fiscal quarter to quarter.

I have no idea what the unemployment rate must be in the countryside. Life is acknowledged to be difficult and from what I can see—it is.

Restaurants have wonderful names: Carpe Diem (the signage is a ying/yang symbol), and Intermezzo (the signage is a man with a 20's slicked back hairdo smoking a cigarette), to name two. Everyone smokes —however, it's not as bad as Asia.

On the way in from the airport, I saw two kinds of arches—McDonalds and, in the next block, a 2000 year old Roman Aqueduct—basic juxtaposition. All the franchises are here—and they are always crowded; Burger King, Pizza Hut, Arby's, etc.

People are fairly well dressed; the Italians have landed and there are many wonderful small shops with fantastically stylish clothes and extraordinary window displays.

Locally manufactured clothing is modestly priced and well made. This is the cold and rainy season(40–50 F), so I bought a nice pair of low Rebok boots (I'm sure they are knock-offs) for about $US14.50. They were made here in Turkey—and exploitive wages were involved, I'm sure.

There are a surprising (to me) number of women (many quite young) wearing headscarves. Of course, this might be because it's Ramadan, but I don't think so. I'll know in three weeks.

Older women seem to be a bit more covered up—with long black coats and sometimes a half-veil covering the lower part of the face. And, at the same time, this is a very modern city and *most* women do not cover themselves in the traditional way.

The call to prayer is heard five times a day—there are so many mosques that you are always within earshot of at least one. A watch is not necessary; one can always figure out what time it is.

I've been to the Sufi Mosque and seen the whirling Dervishes —awesome—and not at all touristy; more like visiting a church or synagogue.

There have been Jews here since the inquisition—I've been to one dusty, crumbling 400 year old synagogue (the 'main' synagogue). There is an Anglican church on the main shopping street.

Food is inexpensive and truly great; the currency is crazy—look up the exchange for today. Everyone in Turkey is a millionaire.

Inflation is not under control (currently about 12% a year), and for the ordinary residents of Istanbul—life is a difficult financial hassle; salaries do not fluctuation with the inflation rate.

Work is not what I expected (what else is new!) and okay. I'm reworking (not re-writing) an adaptation of a Business English curriculum—they want it to sound 'more American' —not very exciting and not much of a challenge.

However, I do have two Business English students. They are very interesting people. Both have visited the U.S. (one to San Francisco and Seattle, the other to Atlanta). They've traveled almost everywhere in Eastern and Western Europe; one has been to South Africa. They both work in the private sector (one for Shell, and the other for a Turkish insurance company). We talk about travel and they are teaching me a lot.

My Turkish colleagues have wonderful senses of humor and know all the special nooks and crannies of the city—

nightlife is, predictably, rather European—small cafes where people sit and eat and drink for hours, music, low tables, the sound of laughter, many languages. Films are plentiful and readily available—the rage this week is the new Matrix movie (not very well received).

Political talk is scarce when Americans are around. I don't know anyone well enough to get a good handle on attitudes —there was a general sigh of relief when the legislature decided not to send troops to Iraq.

Other ex-pats—unremarkable (thus far), and pleasant enough colleagues—five Americans (including two young Black Muslim women from Long Island, who are observing Ramadan), several Canadians, a few Brits, two South Africans (one crazy, one very funny), an Aussie (what environment is complete without at least one?!), and, lastly, one Kiwi.

All for this email. Next time: rugs, or Grand Bazaar, or the Blue Mosque, Kapadokia, and, if you're very good, perhaps a Palace.

Cheers!
Elaine

1 November 2003

From Elaine in Istanbul

The first bomb occurred early in the AM on a Saturday; I was on my way to meet someone. I heard the noise, felt a shock through the air, which was almost immediately filled with dust and flying pieces of stuff, but no glass.

I had no idea what had happened; the infrastructure is so dilapidated here, (this part if the city is at least 8,000 years old), that I thought a gas main (or some other part of the assorted infrastructure that make up a city) had failed. It did not feel like an earthquake.

I went on my way, found a taxi ...

Later that day I learned I'd been about 2 blocks away. The winding labyrinth of streets and alleys protected me from the larger pieces of debris and the glass.

Everyone who is Turkish has rushed to tell me that the perpetrators were not Turkish and had to have come from the outside. Privately, people have told me, that there are Al Queda cells in Istanbul, just waiting for an opportunity. However, they all think that the American Counsel would have been a more likely target.

(The American Counsel, by the way, is an embarrassment of a fortress. I've seen it from a bus. YUK!)

The second bomb DID feel like an earthquake and I immediately got into a doorway. The glass, etc, went flying by ... a few minutes later I saw people with bloody faces, heard a lot of screaming, and knew it was another bomb.

Since then, the streets and alleys—and every corner—are filled with police and army people. Many countries have counsels (the embassies are in Ankara) in this busy part of town. They have become armed camps. I talked to one Swedish guy who needed to have his passport renewed. A simple procedure that normally takes half an hour took half a day. There are many stories like this. There are check-points on bridges causing traffic jams that cannot be described.

Don't know if I will stay or go—a lot depends on the general atmosphere. Right now it's pretty 'iffy'—lots of police and armed soldiers almost everywhere I go. Although I don't feel at all threatened, I really don't like being in places where people are trying to kill each other.

Apart from my time with a few students, work is not at all a challenge and I should finish the whole project in a few weeks.

And now—the Egyptian (spice) Bazaar.

On the way to the Grand Bazaar one must pass through the Egyptian (spice) Bazaar. The plaque on the wall tells the story: a sultan's mother (sultans' mothers had HUGE power) started the building in the early 1500s. Another sultan's mother completed it in the mid 1600s. It has a high vaulted ceiling down the main 'street' and many smaller (in fact a catacomb) of smaller 'streets' that make it VERY easy to get disoriented and, in fact, lost.

It was crowded the day I went and I'm told that is the general state of affairs—always busy with people buying/ selling/hawking.

Well, to be brief, spices I've never heard of in enormous colorful mounds along with sacks of beans and tea of every description are to be found—all sold by the gram or kilo. Saffron, for example is 12 Million Turkish Lira a kilo; you do the math. Also, nuts and candies of every description tempt from all directions. The odor of the place is intoxicating. I was pretty stoned in about half an hour. I bought 100 grams of pistachios to munch as I walked—they have a different flavor and color than those available in California—somewhat sweeter and they are not salted.

So, I'm still in full swing—moving towards the Grand Bazaar —and expect to get there very soon. That's a promise.

Each night I try a different resturant—the fish and eel here are wonderful—many species I've never tasted before. Plenty of chicken and lamb as well.

Still working my way through the many varieties of Baklava.

All for now.

Cheers! |
Elaine

30 November 2003

98

Kapali Garsi ... the Grand (covered) Bazaar

The Grand (covered) Bazaar was begun in the mid-fourteenth and completed in the early fifteen century. As with the Spice Bazaar, it is the handiwork of various Mothers of Sultans. The site itself was always a regional gathering place for trade and once a terminal of the Silk Road.

Since the middle ages, it has grown, so that now—December, 2003—it takes three or four visits of two or three hours each, to BEGIN to scratch the surface of the place. I have paid two visits and have barely started.

Now, it is the locale where goods of every kind and description are bought, traded, and sold. Foreigners pay the 'tourist' tax. It's the wrong place to buy almost anything, my Turkish colleagues have so cautioned me. That does not distract, one iota, from the splendid and fantastic array of 'stuff' on display.

Literally, everything from everywhere is available. Legendary handmade Turkish rugs of wool, silk and wool, cotton, cotton and wool, cotton and silk ... all using natural dyes are found in abundance. So, too, the imitation junk.

Jewelry, from everywhere in every metal and displaying every stone ... pottery, washing machines, clothing, furniture, lumber, paintings, embroidery, electronics, etc.

Other recent sights:

The Galata tower sits just up the hill from the main Synagogue in Istanbul (one of the two that were bombed). Originally part of a fortification built by the Genoese in 1348, it has over the years been used as a warehouse, a prison, and a fire lookout. Restoration was begun in the mid-sixties and is ongoing.

At the foot of the hill on which the tower sits is the Galata Bridge, with people fishing and selling Rolex watches for 10 million Turkish Lira. On the other end of the bridge is the Spice Bazaar.

Mosques—they are everywhere—are usually very beautifully decorated inside and out. I'm not permitted to go completely inside any mosque. And if I decide to visit the 'public' areas, I must cover my head. I have done this twice. And, while I would never violate the local custom, I really did not like being covered up. It is NOT like wearing a hat. I probably won't do it again.

On the last night of Ramadan, I went to Sultanahmet (a district in the Bosphorus part of the city), and the site of the 'blue' mosque. It is the most important mosque built during the Ottoman Empire and is as spectacular as you have heard – mosaics inside and out in the most striking blue you can imagine. Breathtaking. Begun in 1597 and completed in 1660.

On this special night—which, as you know ends the fast—the park around the mosque is filled with tents, rug and silk merchants, small outdoor restaurants, music, games, and the general atmosphere of a county fair.

This is the only time during the year that the call to prayer is sung live. For the past 50 or so years, it is always a recording —except on this night.

In the moments before the call to prayer, light fades and it becomes so quiet you could hear a pin drop on the damp grass. A wispy fog rolls in, shrouding the six minarets, now lit up, in a blurry haze. The Imam appears

on the top of one of the minarets (reminding me of
Hamlet's ghostly father).

Here is a translation of the call to prayer:

God is great. God is great.
God is great. God is great.

I bear witness that there is none worthy of worship but
God
I bear witness that there is none worthy of worship but
God.

I bear witness that Muhammad is the prophet of God.
I bear witness that Muhammad is the prophet of God.

Come to prayer. Come to prayer.

I have been to the Asian side of Istanbul—it looks like
suburbia anywhere—SUV's, upscale shops, and
expensively dressed arrogant teenagers. Not particularly
interesting.

Wandering around the old parts of the city is appealing.
Down very narrow alleys one can find charming antique
shops, fruit and vegetable pushcarts, hardware goods,
and stores selling knock-offs of software, films, and
music—all side by side.

There is a small subway that doesn't go to very many
places and is not very attractive. (Odd in a city where
there is so much wonderful architecture and so many
beautiful things to look at.)

Getting somewhat lost is fun. All I have to do is hop into
a taxi and say the magic word ' Taksim', which is the
square nearest to my flat.

Oh, yes, finally, an apartment, eer, a flat. By middle-class Istanbul standards, it is palatial. Three bedrooms—one of them like a large closet, one a bit bigger, and one is a reasonable size room. All okay for sleeping, showering, and storing clothes, which is about all I'm using the place for now.

Television in English consists of Europe CNN and BBC Primetime.

Gorgeous rugs everywhere—nice wood floors under them—a kitchen, bath, and a large living room about 20 x 30 with a small dining area, and lovely old furniture very well cared for. Certainly comfortable, and within 10 minutes of almost anywhere I need to go on a regular basis. Housekeeper twice a month for 40 million Turkish Lira, each time—cost shared with my flat-mate—a nice young woman from South Africa, who is here teaching English.

For those of you still concerned, the flat is a 5 walk from the British Counsel and maybe 10 minutes from the main Istanbul Synagogue, that were the sites of 2 of the 3 bombings—yes, in the neighborhood.

Things are still rather tense; armed cops and soldiers everywhere, causing traffic jams and general inconvenience for everyone.

I will allow none of it to detract from my exploration of this historic, fabulous, and totally fantastic city; I am treating it all as part of the experience.

Many of you have written to express your concern for my safety. While I appreciate your concern, ... I will allow none of it!...

All for this time.

Cheers!
Elaine

15 December 2003

GLOSSARY

A4   a paper size (8.27x11.69 inches) standard in Europe, Asia, and Latin America

concurrent development   the process of developing a product at several levels to speed internationalization

globalization   creating products for specific world markets

internationalization   the process of removing all cultural context from a program or document

enabilization   the process of implementing the localization process

DTP   electronic desktop publishing using publishing/layout software

icons   pictographic representations

instructional design   the process by which information is systematically mapped, categorized, and organized to facilitate the transmission of information or skills

ISO 9000   ISO (International Organization for Standardization) is a European community-inspired quality inspection and certification program

laser proofs   laser printer output of each page of a document or brochure provided to editors for final corrections prior to going to Lino (see Linotronic below)

linguistic variables   includes the official language(s) of the target country
are your readers mono, bi-, or multi-lingual, and highly educated or basically literate?

localization   a process, the goal of which is to create a document that looks and feels as though it was created in the target country or market

marketing collateral   the material used to market a product or service as distinct from the documentation which is part of the product

mechanicals   non-electronic items provided to a print vendor (such as Lino film, RC paper, pasted-up boards) to create the final printing

modules   individual units of information or instruction
platform compatibility used to describe software that can be used on more than one kind of computer

screen shots a "snapshot" of a computer's screen picture, which is then electronically saved and can be printed in user documentation

simplified English an English with reduced vocabulary (800 plus words)

soy ink non-petroleum based ink, non-toxic and biodegradable

syllabary sets of the written signs (or characters) of a language representing syllables

target market the market to which your product and documentation is directed

text swell the increase in word count when expressing the same idea, concept, or thought from one language to another in a written communication

verifier editor

ABOUT THE AUTHORS

Robert G. Sellin

is a founder and partner in the translation firm:

OSTrans, LLC.
1950 Addison Street, Suite 101
Berkeley, CA 94704
1-800-803-9896
1-510-843-5600

http://www.ostrans.com
rsellin@ostrans.com and sellin1@yahoo.com

Robert is a professional in the field of cross-cultural communication and language translation. His languages are English, German, Spanish, and Portuguese. He has lived, studied and/or worked in Mexico, Germany, Chile, and Brazil. His experience spans over forty years.

Elaine Winters

has lived and worked in Asia, Europe, North America, and the South Pacific.

1525 Spruce Street, Suite 35
Berkeley, CA 94709-1559, U.S.A.
1-510-843-0909

http://www.ewinters.com
ewinters@ewinters.com

With a background in the public and private (corporate and Fortune 500) sectors (domestically and internationally), academia, and the U.S. Peace Corps (Fiji), **Elaine** brings a substantial career of adaptation and adjustment across a spectrum of environments.

Her corporate/academic clients include: Apple, Berlitz, City of Berkeley, Fujian Teachers University, Hong Kong Museum of Science and Technology, Nokia, Nortel, Shaklee Corporation, University of California @ Berkeley, Voluntary Hospitals of America, and both Wells Fargo Bank and Wells Fargo Mortgage Company. Elaine, has been honored with writing awards, presented at conferences, internationally and domestically, and is published in peer reviewed journals. More is available on her website.

INDEX

A

B

C

D

E

F

I

P

R

S

W